BE YOURSELF!

BE YOURSELF!

Based on the comic strip, PEANUTS,
by Charles M. Schulz

RP|KIDS
PHILADELPHIA • LONDON

Library of Congress Control Number: 2012951192

9 8 7 6 5 4 3 2 1
Digit on the right indicates the number of this printing

Art Adapted by Tom Brannon
Designed by Frances J. Soo Ping Chow and Susan Van Horn
Edited by Marlo Scrimizzi
Typography: Agenda and Billy

This special edition was printed for Kohl's Department Stores, Inc.
(for distribution on behalf of Kohl's Cares, LLC, its wholly owned subsidiary)
Published by Running Press Kids
An Imprint of Running Press Book Publishers
A Member of the Perseus Books Group
2300 Chestnut Street
Philadelphia, PA 19103-4371

Kohl's
ISBN 978-0-7624-5146-3
123386
First Edition Printed 04/13–09/13

Visit us on the web!
www.runningpress.com
www.Snoopy.com
www.Kohls.com/Cares

Just like Charlie Brown, Snoopy, Linus, Lucy,
and the WHOLE Peanuts gang, you can be the best
person you can be. Let yourself shine.

BE YOURSELF!

BE A
FRIEND

FRIENDS LIKE SNOOPY COME TO THE RESCUE!

Marcie counts on
her friend Peppermint Patty
IN TOUGH SITUATIONS.

BE LOVING

Lucy is
SCHROEDER'S
#1 FAN.

Snoopy the
AFFECTIONATE BEAGLE
is at it again!

SMOOCH!

Snoopy and Charlie Brown
are made for each other.

Linus and his blanket:
LOVE AT FIRST SQUEEZE.

BE
DETERMINED

HERE COMES
CHARLIE BROWN. . . .

Try again,
Charlie Brown!

Good grief.

BE
HELPFUL

Lucy the expert can
SOLVE ANY PROBLEM.

This beagle will always
LEND A HELPING EAR.

BE
ACTIVE

Snoopy and Linus
go head to head!

And they're off . . .

We have a
WINNER!

One … two … three …   Let's tee off!

Kick that football clear to the moon,
Charlie Brown!

BE
CREATIVE

This creative beagle never has
TOO MUCH INSPIRATION.

BELIEVE

BE YOURSELF!